A Robot Wrote This Book:

Ink and the Algorithm

INTRODUCTION

In the age of AI, we find ourselves witnessing a profound transformation in the world of writing and literature. The emergence of artificial intelligence, or AI, has brought about an unprecedented shift in how we produce, consume, and interact with written content. From chatbots that answer customer inquiries to algorithms that generate news articles and novels, the boundaries of what is possible in the realm of writing have expanded far beyond what was once imagined. Welcome to "A Robot Wrote This Book!", a journey into the exciting, sometimes controversial, and undeniably revolutionary world of AI-authored literature.

The AI revolution didn't happen overnight. It has been a gradual process, marked by incremental advancements that have culminated in AI becoming an integral part of our daily lives. In the beginning, AI was often associated with chatbots and simple automated responses. These early AI systems aimed to mimic human conversation and provide users with basic information or assistance. The famous Turing Test, proposed by Alan Turing in 1950, became a milestone for evaluating AI's capability to imitate human conversation convincingly. As we delve into the world of AI writing, it's essential to recognize that its roots are intertwined with these early endeavors to create AI that can communicate effectively.

At the heart of our exploration lies the concept of AI writing. But what exactly is AI writing? It involves the use of artificial intelligence, particularly natural language processing (NLP) techniques, to generate human-like text. AI systems are trained on massive datasets of text to learn grammar, style, and context, allowing them to generate coherent and contextually relevant content. This definition encompasses a wide range of applications, from auto-generating news articles, poetry, or even writing entire books, as you'll discover in this journey.

To understand where AI writing stands today, we must trace its evolution. One of the most significant breakthroughs occurred with the development of NLP technologies. NLP is a field of AI that focuses on the interaction between humans and computers through natural language. It has evolved from rule-based systems to statistical models and, more recently, neural networks. These neural networks have given rise to advanced language models like GPT-3, which are capable of generating remarkably human-like text. In essence, AI writing is the culmination of decades of research and technological advancement in AI and NLP.

As we venture further into this book, we'll explore the capabilities and limitations of AI writing, its impact on industries ranging from marketing to journalism, and the ethical considerations that accompany this transformative technology. We'll also consider how AI can enhance human creativity, the collaboration between humans and machines, and the myriad of possibilities that AI offers in the world of literature and communication.

Join us on this fascinating journey through "A Robot Wrote This Book!" as we delve deeper into the AI writing revolution, its implications for writers and industries, and the exciting prospects it holds for the future. In the chapters to come, we will explore the inner workings of AI writing, the ethical challenges it presents, and the practical ways in which AI is changing the writing process. So, fasten your seatbelts as we embark on this captivating exploration of AI writing, where creativity meets computation, and the written word is transformed by the digital pen of artificial intelligence.

CONTENTS

1. THE BIRTH OF AI AUTHORS

The concept of AI-generated writing, which has taken centre stage in recent years, is not a sudden revelation. It has deep roots that extend back to the early days of artificial intelligence research, where scientists and engineers were captivated by the idea of machines that could understand and generate human language. In "The Birth of AI Authors," we will embark on a journey through the annals of AI history, exploring the evolution of this extraordinary field and its transformation into a realm where machines can craft literature that challenges our perception of creativity.

1.1 The Turing Test and Early AI Attempts

Our journey begins with the groundbreaking ideas of Alan Turing. In 1950, Turing introduced the Turing Test, a concept that sought to determine whether a machine could exhibit intelligent behaviour indistinguishable from that of a human. The Turing Test was a pivotal moment in the history of AI, as it set the stage for defining the capabilities and limitations of artificial intelligence.

Early AI attempts to pass the Turing Test focused on creating chatbots and expert systems that could engage in conversations and provide information. While these early attempts were primitive compared to today's AI models, they laid the foundation for the development of natural language processing (NLP) and AI writing. The notion that machines could understand and generate human language began to take shape.

1.2 Natural Language Processing (NLP): The Foundation of AI Writing

The evolution of AI writing is intimately tied to the growth of natural language processing (NLP). NLP is a branch of artificial intelligence that focuses on enabling computers to understand, interpret, and generate human language. In the early years, NLP systems relied on rule-based approaches, where explicit instructions were used to process language. However, these rule-based systems had limitations, as they struggled to adapt to the complexities and nuances of human language.

Advancements in machine learning and statistical modelling brought a significant shift in NLP research. Instead of relying on predefined rules, researchers began to develop systems that could learn from large datasets of text. This change marked the transition from rule-based NLP to data-driven approaches, which allowed computers to capture the subtleties of language more effectively.

1.3 GPT-3 and Beyond: The State of the Art in AI Text Generation

One of the most remarkable breakthroughs in AI writing is the advent of powerful language models like GPT-3 (Generative Pre-trained Transformer 3). GPT-3, developed by OpenAI, is a neural network-based model that has garnered attention for its ability to generate coherent and contextually relevant text. It stands as a testament to the progress made in the field of AI writing and NLP.

GPT-3 and similar models have achieved human-level performance in various language tasks, including text generation, translation, and question answering. These models are pre-trained on massive amounts of text data, which allows them to understand context, grammar, and style, making them capable of producing text that appears convincingly human-written. The possibilities for AI writing continue to expand as researchers work on even more advanced models.

As we continue our exploration of AI writing in the following chapters, we will delve into the inner workings of AI systems, how they learn from text corpora, and the fine-tuning process that tailors these models for specific writing tasks. We'll also examine the ethical considerations surrounding AI-generated content and how AI writing has evolved to become a transformative force in literature and communication. Join us in the next chapter as we explore the fascinating landscape of AI text generation, where machines write with astonishing creativity and fluency.

2. Behind the Scenes of AI Writing

In the previous chapters, we explored the evolution of AI writing and its roots in the early days of artificial intelligence. Now, let's journey behind the scenes to understand the inner workings of AI writing. How do machines, particularly advanced language models like GPT-3, generate human-like text that often seems indistinguishable from what a human would produce? This chapter will provide a comprehensive look into the technology that powers AI writing.

2.1 How AI Models Learn from Text Corpora

At the heart of AI writing lies the ability of machines to learn from vast amounts of text data. To achieve this, AI models are trained on massive text corpora, which are extensive collections of written material from books, articles, websites, and more. The idea is simple but powerful: by exposing the model to an enormous and diverse range of text, it can learn patterns, grammar, vocabulary, and context, much like a human would.

These text corpora encompass a broad spectrum of languages, topics, and writing styles. By analysing this diverse range of material, AI models gain an understanding of how language works, from the intricacies of grammar to the nuances of word usage. They learn to recognize patterns, relationships between words, and even cultural and contextual factors that influence language.

2.2 The Role of Neural Networks

Neural networks are the backbone of AI writing. These computational structures are inspired by the human brain and are composed of layers of interconnected nodes, or neurons. In the context of AI writing, they are specifically designed to process language.

The key to understanding how neural networks function in AI writing is to consider them as pattern recognition machines. They receive input data, process it through multiple layers, and make predictions or generate text based on the learned patterns. The deeper and more complex the neural network, the better it can capture intricate patterns and context in language.

Neural networks are crucial in deciphering context, style, and semantics, allowing AI models to generate coherent and contextually relevant text. The combination of vast training data and sophisticated neural networks is what gives AI writing its power.

2.3 Fine-Tuning Models for Specific Tasks

While training AI models on vast text corpora forms the foundation, fine-tuning is the process that tailors these models for specific writing tasks. In essence, fine-tuning adapts a pre-trained model to perform more effectively in particular domains or tasks. For example, fine-tuning a model for medical writing would involve training it on a dataset containing medical literature, enabling it to generate specialized content.

This fine-tuning process is a critical aspect of AI writing. It takes the general knowledge and language understanding acquired during the initial training phase and customizes it to be more domain-specific. The outcome is an AI model that can excel in generating content relevant to a particular field, making it a versatile tool for various industries.

The synergy of training on diverse text corpora, utilizing advanced neural networks, and fine-tuning models for specific tasks is what empowers AI writing to generate content that is not only coherent and contextually relevant but also tailored to specific needs.

3. Potato The Good, the Bad, and the Biased

As we venture deeper into the landscape of AI writing, it becomes imperative to address the ethical considerations and challenges that accompany the generation of content by artificial intelligence. In "The Good, the Bad, and the Biased," we delve into the multifaceted impact of AI-generated text on society, exploring the positive contributions, the potential pitfalls, and the persistent issue of bias.

3.1 AI Ethics and Bias in Writing

The ethical dimensions of AI writing extend beyond the realm of technology and touch upon fundamental principles of fairness, transparency, and accountability. As AI models process vast amounts of data, they may inadvertently perpetuate or even amplify existing biases present in the training data. This raises concerns about the fairness and impartiality of AI-generated content.

Addressing bias in AI writing involves a careful examination of the training data and the implementation of mechanisms to mitigate and correct biases. Developers and researchers are actively working to create AI systems that not only generate high-quality content but also adhere to ethical standards, promoting inclusivity and fairness.

3.2 The Impact of AI-Generated Text on Society

The proliferation of AI-generated text has wide-ranging consequences for society. On the positive side, AI can enhance efficiency and productivity in content creation, providing valuable support to writers and content creators. However, the widespread use of AI writing tools also raises questions about the potential displacement of human writers in certain industries.

In journalism, for example, AI algorithms can rapidly generate news articles based on data and events. While this can increase the speed of news dissemination, it challenges traditional journalistic practices and raises concerns about the authenticity and reliability of AI-generated news.

3.3 Content Moderation and AI

With the exponential growth of online content, content moderation has become a critical concern. AI plays a significant role in automating content moderation tasks, identifying and filtering out inappropriate or harmful content. However, the challenge lies in ensuring that AI algorithms can accurately discern context, understanding the subtleties of language and cultural nuances to avoid false positives or negatives.

Efforts are underway to strike a balance between the benefits of automated content moderation and the potential risks associated with overreliance on AI systems. Achieving an effective and fair content moderation process involves continuous refinement and adaptation of AI models to the evolving landscape of online communication.

3.4 The Ongoing Debate Over AI Ethics

The intersection of AI and ethics has sparked ongoing debates within the tech community, academia, and society at large. Questions about accountability, transparency, and the societal impact of AI-generated content continue to be subjects of rigorous discussion. As the capabilities of AI writing models evolve, so too must our ethical frameworks and guidelines.

In this chapter, we've touched on the ethical considerations surrounding AI writing, including the potential for bias, the societal impact, and the challenges of content moderation. In the subsequent chapters, we will explore the collaborative potential between humans and machines in the writing process, the transformations occurring in various industries, and the creative possibilities that arise when AI and human authors join forces.

4. Collaboration between Humans and Machines

In the evolving landscape of writing, a compelling narrative is emerging—one of collaboration between humans and machines. As we explore the synergies between artificial intelligence and human creativity, we unveil a new chapter in the history of literature. "Collaboration between Humans and Machines" delves into the ways AI is not just a tool for writers but a creative partner, challenging our traditional notions of authorship.

4.1 Human-AI Collaboration in Writing

The traditional image of a solitary writer hunched over a typewriter is evolving into a dynamic collaboration between human authors and AI. Writing tools powered by artificial intelligence offer more than just grammar and style suggestions; they actively contribute to the creative process. Human-AI collaboration in writing is not about replacement but enhancement. AI becomes a thinking companion, suggesting ideas, providing inspiration, and refining drafts.

Writers can harness the efficiency of AI to overcome creative blocks, explore new perspectives, and iterate through countless possibilities. The fusion of human intuition and the computational power of AI opens new horizons in creativity, transforming the writing process into a collaborative and dynamic endeavor.

4.2 Creative Partnerships: AI as a Co-Author

Beyond assistance, AI is stepping into the role of a co-author. The concept of AI as a creative partner is exemplified by projects where AI systems contribute significantly to the content creation process. From generating poetry to crafting entire novels, AI is proving its ability to coalesce words into art.

This collaborative model challenges our traditional understanding of authorship. When an AI system contributes ideas, themes, and even entire sections to a piece of writing, questions arise about the attribution of creative work. Who is the author when the lines between human and machine contributions blur?

4.3 The Future of Writing Teams

As AI continues to integrate into the writing process, the concept of a writing team is undergoing a transformation. These teams, once comprised solely of human writers and editors, now include AI as a valuable team member. In this evolving landscape, writers collaborate not just with other humans but with intelligent algorithms that offer unique insights and augment the creative process.

The future promises writing teams where the strengths of both humans and AI are leveraged to produce content that is not only efficient but also imbued with a blend of human creativity and machine intelligence. The synergy between human intuition and AI algorithms gives rise to a powerful force that can transcend the limitations of individual creativity.

4.4 Embracing the Collaborative Paradigm

The collaboration between humans and machines is not a threat to the traditional craft of writing but an opportunity for its evolution. Writers who embrace this collaborative paradigm find themselves at the forefront of a literary renaissance, where the boundaries of creativity are expanded by the capabilities of AI.

As we progress through this book, we will explore further how AI is impacting various industries, from marketing to publishing. We will also dive into the creative realms of AI-generated novels and poetry.

5. The Implications for Writers

As the symbiotic relationship between humans and AI in writing continues to evolve, writers find themselves at a crossroads—facing both challenges and opportunities. "The Implications for Writers" explores how AI writing tools are reshaping the landscape of creativity and storytelling. From the transformation of the writing process to addressing concerns about intellectual property, this chapter delves into the multifaceted impact of AI on the craft of writing.

5.1 How AI Writing Tools Are Changing the Writing Process

AI writing tools have become indispensable companions for many writers, offering a suite of functionalities that extend beyond basic grammar and spell checks. From suggesting alternative word choices to helping refine the overall structure of a piece, these tools contribute to a more streamlined and efficient writing process.

Writers can leverage AI to overcome common challenges, such as writer's block, by providing prompts and generating ideas. The instant feedback from AI tools allows for rapid iteration and refinement, turning the writing process into a more dynamic and collaborative endeavour.

5.2 Copyright and Plagiarism Concerns

The integration of AI into the writing process raises important questions about copyright and intellectual property. As AI systems generate content autonomously, issues of ownership and attribution become more complex. Who owns the rights to a piece of writing when AI is a co-author or the primary content creator?

The challenge extends to concerns about potential plagiarism. With AI's ability to generate diverse and contextually relevant content, the lines between original work and AI-generated content can blur. Writers and content creators must navigate this intricate landscape, demanding a revaluation of existing copyright frameworks.

5.3 Adapt or Perish: The Writer's Response to AI

In the face of these transformative changes, writers are presented with a clear choice—adapt or perish. The integration of AI into the writing process is not a replacement but an augmentation of human creativity. Writers who embrace AI tools as collaborators rather than competitors find themselves better equipped to navigate the evolving demands of the industry.

Adaptation involves not only mastering the use of AI writing tools but also understanding their limitations. Writers retain the unique ability to infuse their work with emotions, personal experiences, and cultural nuances that AI, as of now, struggles to replicate authentically.

5.4 The Ethical Writer in the Age of AI

In navigating the implications of AI, writers must also consider the ethical dimensions of their craft. As AI-generated content becomes more prevalent, writers bear the responsibility of ensuring transparency and authenticity in their work. Disclosing the involvement of AI in the creative process becomes a crucial aspect of maintaining ethical standards and fostering trust with readers.

Moreover, the ethical writer embraces the collaborative potential of AI while remaining vigilant against biases embedded in training data. Writers must actively participate in shaping the ethical guidelines governing AI writing, advocating for fairness, inclusivity, and responsible content creation.

5.5 Harnessing AI's Creative Potential

Rather than viewing AI as a threat, writers can harness its creative potential to explore new frontiers in storytelling. The fusion of human imagination and machine intelligence opens doors to innovative narrative structures, interactive storytelling experiences, and the creation of content that transcends traditional boundaries.

Writers who approach AI with an open mind and a willingness to experiment find themselves at the forefront of a literary renaissance. The potential for groundbreaking collaborations, unique narrative forms, and the democratization of storytelling tools places writers in a position to shape the future of literature.

As we progress through this exploration of AI writing, subsequent chapters will delve into the impact on various industries, the creative intersections of AI and literature, and the fascinating realm of AI-generated novels and poetry. Join us as we continue to unravel the dynamic relationship between humans and machines in the ever-evolving narrative of the written word.

6. INDUSTRIES TRANSFORMED

The impact of AI-generated content extends far beyond the realm of individual writers; it reverberates through entire industries, reshaping the way content is produced, disseminated, and consumed. In "Industries Transformed," we explore how AI is revolutionizing marketing, advertising, journalism, publishing, and self-publishing, leaving an indelible mark on the landscape of written communication.

6.1 AI-Generated Content in Marketing and Advertising

In the world of marketing and advertising, the demand for engaging and personalized content is incessant. AI has emerged as a formidable ally, enabling the creation of compelling advertisements, product descriptions, and marketing copy. Chatbots powered by AI engage with customers, providing instant responses and product recommendations, enhancing the overall customer experience.

Personalization is a key strength of AI, allowing marketers to tailor content based on user behaviour, preferences, and demographic information. From email campaigns to social media posts, AI-driven tools analyse data to deliver content that resonates with specific target audiences, optimizing engagement and conversion rates.

6.2 Journalism and News Automation

The fast-paced nature of journalism is well-suited to the capabilities of AI. News organizations are increasingly utilizing AI algorithms to generate news articles quickly and efficiently. Automated journalism systems can process vast amounts of data, distilling complex information into coherent and timely news reports.

While AI streamlines the news production process, it also raises questions about journalistic integrity and the potential for bias in automated reporting. Striking a balance between speed and accuracy is an ongoing challenge as newsrooms grapple with incorporating AI into their editorial workflows.

6.3 The Impact on Publishing and Self-Publishing

The publishing industry has undergone significant transformations with the advent of AI. Traditional publishers are using AI to analyse market trends, predict book sales, and identify potential bestsellers.

On the other hand, self-published authors are leveraging AI writing tools to enhance their creative process, streamline editing, and reach wider audiences.

AI-driven recommendation algorithms play a crucial role in guiding readers to discover new books based on their preferences. The democratization of publishing facilitated by self-publishing platforms, combined with AI tools, empowers authors to bring their stories to the forefront without traditional gatekeepers.

6.4 Challenges and Opportunities in Publishing

While AI presents numerous opportunities in publishing, it also introduces challenges. The rise of AI-generated content poses questions about originality, authorship, and the role of human creativity. Publishers are tasked with navigating these complexities, establishing guidelines for the ethical use of AI in content creation and preserving the authenticity of literary works.

Despite these challenges, AI offers valuable insights into reader behaviour and preferences, enabling publishers to optimize their marketing strategies and tailor their catalogues to meet evolving demands. The dynamic interplay between human creativity and AI-generated content is shaping a new era in publishing.

6.5 The Transformative Power of Self-Publishing

Self-publishing, empowered by AI writing tools, has become a force to be reckoned with. Authors no longer depend solely on traditional publishing channels; they can independently create, publish, and market their works to a global audience. AI assists in the editing process, suggests improvements, and even generates promotional materials, providing self-published authors with a suite of tools to enhance their professional capabilities.

The transformative power of self-publishing extends beyond literature, reaching into other creative domains such as music, art, and niche markets. As AI continues to evolve, self-publishing becomes an increasingly viable avenue for creative expression and entrepreneurship.

In the chapters that follow, we will delve deeper into the creative realms of AI, exploring its impact on art and music composition, its intersection with literature, and the fascinating world of AI-generated novels and poetry.

7. The Creative Machine

From visual masterpieces to musical symphonies and the crafting of entire novels, this chapter explores the evolving relationship between machines and creativity.

7.1 AI in Art and Visual Composition

AI has made significant strides in the realm of visual arts, challenging conventional notions of artistic creation. Generative models, driven by neural networks, analyse patterns in vast datasets of visual art to create entirely new compositions. AI-generated art ranges from paintings and drawings to digital and interactive installations.

Artistic collaborations between human creators and AI algorithms have produced works that push the boundaries of imagination. The melding of human intent with the computational capabilities of AI introduces a new dimension to the art world, sparking discussions about authorship, inspiration, and the very nature of creativity.

7.2 The Intersection of AI and Literature

In the realm of literature, AI's influence extends beyond assisting writers in the creative process. Literary works generated entirely by AI challenge our preconceptions about storytelling and the role of human imagination. AI models like GPT-3 have demonstrated the ability to craft coherent narratives, generating prose that, in some instances, is indistinguishable from human-authored content.

While the debate over the authenticity of AI-generated literature continues, these experiments serve as a testament to the evolving capabilities of artificial intelligence in the creative realm. As AI authors become more proficient, they invite us to reevaluate our understanding of storytelling and the essence of narrative art.

7.3 AI-Generated Novels and Poetry

AI-generated novels and poetry are captivating examples of machines expressing creativity in written form. Projects where entire novels or collections of poems are authored by AI raise intriguing questions about the nature of storytelling and poetic expression. Can a machine truly understand the depth of human emotions and the nuances of language required to create compelling literature?

While AI-generated novels may lack the personal experiences and emotional depth inherent in human-authored works, they offer a glimpse into a future where machines contribute to the rich tapestry of literary expression. The coexistence of human and AI-authored literature prompts reflection on the diverse ways in which stories can be told and shared.

7.4 Exploring Creative Frontiers in Music Composition

In the realm of music composition, AI algorithms are composing symphonies, generating melodies, and producing pieces that captivate listeners. The ability of AI to analyse vast musical datasets and emulate various styles allows for the creation of music that spans genres and eras.

Collaborations between composers and AI systems showcase the potential for innovative musical expressions. AI-generated compositions challenge traditional notions of artistic authorship, prompting musicians and audiences alike to reconsider the boundaries of creativity and the sources of musical inspiration.

7.5 The Ethical Dimensions of AI Creativity

As AI steps into the realm of creative expression, ethical considerations come to the forefront. Questions about the attribution of creative works, the impact on employment in creative industries, and the potential loss of a human touch in art and literature need careful examination.

The ethical use of AI in the creative process involves acknowledging the contributions of both human and machine creators. Striking a balance between technological advancement and ethical considerations is imperative to ensure that the integration of AI enhances, rather than diminishes, the richness of human creativity.

In the upcoming chapters, we will explore the road ahead for AI writing, including the development of GPT-4 and the potential future advancements in AI writing technology.

8. The Road Ahead

As we stand at the crossroads of artificial intelligence and creative expression, the road ahead beckons with promise and uncertainty. "The Road Ahead" invites us to peer into the future of AI writing technology, exploring the possibilities, challenges, and ethical considerations that lie on the horizon.

8.1 GPT-4 and Beyond

The next milestone on the horizon is GPT-4, the successor to the already groundbreaking GPT-3. As technology advances, we can anticipate even more sophisticated language models with enhanced capabilities. GPT-4 is expected to exhibit a deeper understanding of context, refine its ability to emulate various writing styles, and potentially even venture into realms of creativity yet unexplored.

With each iteration, AI writing technology is poised to become an even more integral part of our daily lives. From generating text for diverse industries to offering creative assistance to writers and artists, GPT-4 and its successors hold the potential to further blur the lines between human and machine creativity.

8.2 The Promise of Enhanced Creativity

The road ahead is marked by the promise of enhanced creativity facilitated by AI. Writers will find themselves armed with ever-more-sophisticated tools that understand context, tone, and intent. Creativity will be amplified, not replaced, as AI assists in ideation, suggests plot twists, and contributes to the tapestry of human expression.

In the world of literature, AI may not only generate text but inspire entirely new genres and narrative forms. The collaborative potential between human authors and advanced AI models opens avenues for storytelling that transcend the boundaries of traditional genres, offering readers an immersive and diverse literary experience.

8.3 Ethical Considerations in AI Writing

As we journey into the future, the ethical considerations surrounding AI writing become increasingly paramount. Transparency in disclosing AI involvement in creative works, ensuring fairness in representation, and addressing biases in training data will be crucial. A proactive approach to establishing ethical guidelines will be essential to navigate the evolving landscape of AI and creativity.

The responsibility falls on developers, writers, and policymakers alike to strike a balance between technological advancement and ethical stewardship. Collaborative efforts are needed to ensure that AI enhances the creative process without compromising the authenticity, diversity, and ethical integrity of human expression.

8.4 The Evolution of Human-AI Collaboration

The collaborative paradigm between humans and AI will continue to evolve. As AI writing technology becomes more sophisticated, the creative relationship between human authors and machines will deepen. Writers will increasingly view AI not as a mere tool but as a partner in the creative process, contributing unique perspectives, insights, and even elements of surprise.

This evolution will extend beyond individual authors to encompass collaborative writing teams, where humans and AI collaborate seamlessly to produce content that resonates with audiences. The fusion of human intuition, emotion, and creativity with the analytical and generative capacities of AI promises a new era of literary and artistic exploration.

8.5 Navigating Challenges: Job Displacement and Adaptation

The road ahead is not without its challenges. The potential for job displacement in certain sectors of the writing and creative industries raises concerns about the future of employment. Writers and creatives must adapt to the changing landscape, acquiring new skills, and embracing the collaborative potential of AI to remain at the forefront of their crafts.

Education and training programs will play a crucial role in preparing the next generation of writers for a future where AI is an integral part of the creative toolkit. Embracing lifelong learning and staying abreast of technological advancements will be essential for writers to thrive in the evolving ecosystem of AI and creativity.

8.6 Embracing the Uncharted

One thing remains certain—AI will continue to reshape the landscape of creative expression. The uncharted territories of AI-generated novels, poetry, art, and music beckon writers and artists to explore, experiment, and redefine the boundaries of their craft.

The road ahead is an invitation to embrace the unknown, to envision a future where the collaboration between human creativity and artificial intelligence leads to innovations that transcend our current understanding of literature and art. It is a journey into a realm where the creative machine and the human artist coexist, each contributing to the vibrant mosaic of human expression.

9. Navigating the Creative Horizon

As we approach the final stretch of our exploration into the synergy of human creativity and artificial intelligence, we find ourselves at the threshold of a creative horizon. "Navigating the Creative Horizon" delves into practical insights, considerations, and tips for writers seeking to navigate the ever-expanding landscape shaped by AI-assisted creativity.

9.1 Embracing AI as a Creative Tool

AI is not a replacement for human creativity; rather, it is a powerful tool that can augment and amplify the creative process. Writers are encouraged to embrace AI as a creative ally, a collaborator that can provide inspiration, overcome creative blocks, and offer fresh perspectives.

Consider incorporating AI writing tools into your creative toolkit. Experiment with different platforms and models to discover how they align with your unique writing style and preferences. From grammar checks to ideation assistance, AI tools can streamline aspects of the writing process, allowing you to focus more on the expressive and imaginative dimensions of your work.

9.2 Leveraging AI for Ideation and Inspiration

One of the notable strengths of AI lies in its capacity to generate ideas and offer creative prompts. When facing writer's block or seeking novel concepts, AI can be a valuable resource. Many platforms allow you to input prompts or themes, and the AI responds with suggestions that can spark your creativity.

As a writer, leverage this capability by exploring unexpected ideas generated by AI. Use them as starting points, allowing your own unique voice and perspective to shape and expand upon the generated content. The fusion of AI-driven inspiration with human ingenuity can lead to unexpected and compelling creative outcomes.

9.3 Ethical Considerations in AI-Augmented Writing

Navigating the creative horizon with AI involves a mindful approach to ethics. Writers should be aware of the potential biases in AI models and the implications of using AI-generated content. Transparency is key—consider informing your audience if AI tools played a role in your creative process, fostering trust and transparency.

Additionally, actively engage in discussions about ethical considerations in AI and writing. Contribute to the development of guidelines and standards that promote responsible AI use in creative endeavours. By being conscious of the ethical dimensions, writers play a crucial role in shaping a future where AI and human creativity coexist harmoniously.

9.4 Balancing Automation and Personal Expression

While AI excels at automating certain aspects of writing, maintaining a balance between automation and personal expression is paramount. Avoid over-reliance on AI for creative decisions that are inherently human, such as expressing emotions, personal experiences, or cultural nuances. Your unique voice and perspective are irreplaceable aspects of your creative identity.

Consider using AI tools as assistants rather than decision-makers. Allow them to enhance your efficiency in areas like grammar and style checks but reserve the final creative decisions for your intuition and artistic sensibility. This balance ensures that AI supports your creative process without overshadowing your individuality as a writer.

9.5 Lifelong Learning and Adaptation

As the creative horizon continues to evolve, embrace the ethos of lifelong learning. Stay informed about advancements in AI writing technology, new models, and emerging trends. Adaptation is key to thriving in the dynamic landscape of AI and creativity.

Participate in workshops, attend conferences, and explore educational opportunities that provide insights into the intersection of AI and writing. Continuous learning enables writers to stay at the forefront of the field, equipped with the knowledge and skills needed to navigate the evolving creative landscape.

9.6 The Enduring Role of Human Creativity

Ultimately, the enduring role of human creativity remains central to the narrative of writing. AI is a tool, a collaborator, but it is the human touch that infuses writing with emotions, experiences, and the essence of the human condition. As we venture into the creative horizon shaped by AI, writers play a pivotal role in steering the course and preserving the authenticity of creative expression.

10. CRAFTING TOMORROW'S NARRATIVES

10.1 Dynamic Storytelling with AI

The future of storytelling is dynamic, and AI stands at the forefront of this transformation. Imagine narratives that adapt in real-time based on reader interactions, preferences, and even cultural contexts. AI can contribute to the creation of interactive, personalized storytelling experiences that captivate audiences in unprecedented ways.

Writers can explore the potential of AI-driven narrative structures, experimenting with branching storylines, alternative endings, and characters that evolve in response to reader choices. This collaborative dance between human creativity and AI algorithms opens up a new frontier in storytelling, where each narrative becomes a unique and interactive journey.

10.2 Multimodal Narratives: Beyond Text

The narrative canvas is expanding beyond traditional text to embrace a multitude of expressive mediums. AI is becoming increasingly proficient in generating content across various modalities, including images, audio, and video. Writers can envision narratives that seamlessly blend text with multimedia elements, creating immersive and engaging storytelling experiences.

Consider exploring projects that incorporate AI-generated visuals or soundscapes to complement your written narratives. This convergence of modalities enriches the storytelling palette, allowing for a more profound emotional impact and a deeper connection with readers.

10.3 AI as a Co-Creator in World-Building

Crafting fictional worlds is a hallmark of imaginative storytelling, and AI can serve as a co-creator in this process. AI models can analyse vast datasets to generate detailed and coherent world-building elements, from intricate landscapes to unique cultures and histories.

Writers can leverage AI to spark inspiration for world-building, using generated content as a foundation to build upon. This collaborative approach allows for the creation of rich, expansive universes that blend the imaginative prowess of human authors with the vast knowledge encapsulated in AI models.

10.4 Tackling Global Challenges Through Narrative

The narratives of tomorrow will grapple with the pressing challenges of our times, from climate change to social justice issues. AI can be a powerful ally in crafting narratives that address these complex and interconnected global themes. Writers can draw on AI-generated insights and data to inform and enrich their storytelling, fostering a deeper understanding of real-world issues.

Consider projects that weave together fictional narratives with factual information and insights provided by AI models. This fusion of creativity and data-driven storytelling has the potential to raise awareness, prompt reflection, and inspire action on a global scale.

10.5 Fostering Inclusivity and Diversity

AI writing tools are not immune to biases present in training data, but writers can actively work to counteract this by promoting inclusivity and diversity in their narratives. Intentionally curate diverse datasets to train AI models, ensuring that characters, perspectives, and cultural nuances are authentically represented.

Writers play a vital role in shaping narratives that celebrate the richness of human experience. By actively engaging with AI in the creation process, authors can contribute to the development of more inclusive and diverse storytelling that resonates with a global audience.

10.6 The Human Touch: Emotions, Nuances, and Creativity

While AI continues to evolve, the human touch remains irreplaceable in storytelling. Emotions, nuances, and the depth of human experience are facets of creativity that machines, as of now, struggle to fully comprehend. Writers should embrace their unique ability to infuse narratives with authenticity, empathy, and the raw essence of humanity.

As we craft tomorrow's narratives in collaboration with AI, let us not forget the enduring power of the human imagination. It is the emotional resonance, the intimate understanding of the human condition, and the capacity to evoke empathy that will continue to distinguish human-authored stories in the ever-expanding realm of AI-assisted creativity.

11. SYNTHESIS AND REFLECTION

11.1 A Tapestry Woven Together

Our exploration has been a journey through diverse realms—AI-assisted writing, collaborative creativity, ethical considerations, and the evolving landscape of literature and art. The threads of human creativity and machine intelligence intertwine to form a tapestry woven with innovation, challenges, and the boundless possibilities of the creative horizon.

In the realm of AI-assisted writing, we witnessed the emergence of tools that go beyond grammar checks, becoming true collaborators in the creative process. From ideation to content generation, these tools have the potential to reshape the writing landscape, offering writers new avenues for exploration.

11.2 Collaborative Creativity: The Dance of Humans and Machines

The dance between human authors and AI is a nuanced interplay of creativity. We explored how AI serves as a thinking companion, a co-author, and a tool that can inspire and augment human creativity. From overcoming writer's block to crafting entire narratives, the collaboration between humans and machines is a testament to the transformative power of partnership.

This collaboration is not without its challenges, especially in navigating ethical considerations and preserving the authenticity of creative expression. As the dance evolves, so too must our understanding of the ethical dimensions surrounding AI-generated content. Writers play a crucial role in shaping guidelines that ensure responsible and transparent use of AI in the creative process.

11.3 The Evolution of Literature and Art

In the expansive realm of literature and art, we witnessed the impact of AI on various industries—marketing, journalism, publishing, and self-publishing. AI has become a force that both challenges traditional norms and opens doors to new possibilities. From news automation to the democratization of publishing through self-publishing platforms, AI is reshaping the landscape of written communication.

AI's influence extends to the creation of visual art, music composition, novels, and poetry. We explored the intersections of AI with different creative domains, raising questions about authorship, originality, and the enduring role of human creativity. The evolving nature of AI-generated content invites us to reevaluate our understanding of storytelling, narrative forms, and the essence of artistic expression.

11.4 The Road Ahead: Navigating Challenges and Embracing Opportunities

As we look to the road ahead, challenges and opportunities coalesce on the horizon. GPT-4 and future iterations promise enhanced creative capabilities, inviting writers to explore new frontiers. Ethical considerations will continue to shape the responsible use of AI, ensuring that creativity is not constrained by biases and that transparency remains a guiding principle.

The enduring role of human creativity is central to the narrative of AI-assisted writing. While machines can automate and assist, the human touch—emotions, nuance, and the depth of experience—remains an irreplaceable aspect of storytelling. Writers are called not just to adapt to technological shifts but to actively participate in shaping a future where the collaborative dance between humans and machines is harmonious and enriching.

11.5 The Writer's Toolkit: Balancing Automation and Individuality

In navigating this transformative landscape, the writer's toolkit expands to include AI as a valuable instrument. Balancing automation and individuality becomes a key consideration. Writers are encouraged to embrace AI tools as collaborators, recognizing their potential to enhance efficiency and spark creativity. However, the preservation of individuality, emotions, and the human essence of storytelling remains paramount.

As writers, you are the architects of the narrative future. Adaptation, lifelong learning, and a thoughtful approach to ethical considerations will be your compass. The synthesis of human and machine creativity is an ongoing dialogue, a narrative that unfolds with each keystroke, each idea generated, and each story crafted.

In the final chapter of "A Robot Wrote This Book!", we will bring our exploration to a close, offering a glimpse into the future of writing, creativity, and the enduring dance between human authors and artificial intelligence. Join us as we bid farewell to this transformative journey and envision the limitless possibilities that await on the horizon of human and machine collaboration.

12. BEYOND BOUNDARIES

As we embark on the final chapter of our exploration, the narrative we've woven through the intersections of artificial intelligence and creative expression approaches its denouement. "Beyond Boundaries" invites us to cast our gaze beyond the confines of the known, embracing the limitless potential that arises when human ingenuity converges with the capabilities of artificial intelligence.

12.1 Uncharted Territories of Creativity

Our journey has been a venture into uncharted territories, where the familiar markers of creativity blur and expand. Artificial intelligence, once viewed as a mere tool, has become a companion in the creative process. It is within these uncharted realms that we glimpse the emergence of novel ideas, unconventional narratives, and unprecedented forms of expression.

As writers stand at the precipice of this unexplored landscape, the potential for innovation and reinvention beckons. The boundaries of storytelling, literature, and art extend further than ever before, inviting authors to push against the edges of convention and explore the vastness of creative possibility.

12.2 The Symphony of Multimodal Expression

Creativity, once confined to the written word, now resonates in a symphony of multimodal expression. The narrative canvas has broadened to include images, audio, and video, with artificial intelligence contributing to the orchestration of this expansive creative symphony. Writers can envision projects that transcend the limitations of traditional mediums, creating immersive experiences that engage audiences on multiple sensory levels.

Consider the fusion of visual elements, soundscapes, and textual narratives to craft stories that transcend the boundaries of conventional storytelling. This multimodal approach provides a tapestry of creative expression that captivates, challenges, and enriches the reader's experience.

12.3 Crafting Narratives Informed by Global Realities

As we peer into the future, the narratives that resonate will be those that grapple with the global realities of our times. Climate change, social justice, and interconnected global challenges form the backdrop against which stories unfold. Artificial intelligence, with its ability to analyse vast datasets and provide insights, becomes a tool for writers to craft narratives that bridge the gap between fiction and the pressing issues of our world.

Writers are called upon to weave stories that inspire empathy, provoke reflection, and prompt action. The collaboration between human creativity and artificial intelligence extends beyond the confines of literary creation to become a catalyst for social consciousness and change.

12.4 The Intersection of Technology and Creativity

Technology and creativity, once perceived as distinct realms, now converge seamlessly. Writers are not just authors; they are architects of immersive experiences, curators of multimedia narratives, and shapers of the evolving landscape of creative expression. Embracing technology is not a concession to modernity but a celebration of the tools that empower writers to navigate the complex currents of the digital age.

Consider the integration of cutting-edge technologies into your creative process—virtual reality, augmented reality, or interactive storytelling platforms. The convergence of technology and creativity opens doors to storytelling experiences that defy traditional boundaries and captivate audiences in unprecedented ways.

12.5 The Essence of Human Creativity

Amidst the technological marvels and AI-assisted ingenuity, the essence of human creativity remains the beating heart of storytelling. Emotions, personal experiences, and the nuances of the human condition are facets of creativity that resonate uniquely with each individual. While machines contribute to the symphony of creativity, it is the human touch that infuses narratives with authenticity and depth.

Writers, armed with the tools of artificial intelligence, navigate the creative landscape with a compass forged from their own experiences, insights, and imaginations. The enduring role of human creativity ensures that each story told, each idea explored, remains a testament to the limitless possibilities of human expression.

12.6 The Ever-Unfolding Story

As we draw the curtains on our exploration, the story does not conclude but evolves. The ever-unfolding narrative of artificial intelligence and creativity is an ongoing dialogue between human authors and the technological tools that accompany them. The possibilities are boundless, and the next chapter is yet to be written.

As writers gaze toward the horizon, they stand on the cusp of an era where the collaboration between human imagination and machine intelligence continues to shape the landscape of storytelling. It is a future where the written word transcends its traditional constraints, where narratives become immersive experiences, and where the human spirit of creativity soars unbounded.

EPILOGUE

As we reflect on the chapters traversed, it becomes clear that this is not the end but a pause in the ever-unfinished symphony of creativity.

The narratives we've explored, the challenges encountered, and the possibilities unveiled are threads woven into the fabric of an ongoing story. The interplay of artificial intelligence and human creativity forms the melody that transcends the boundaries of tradition and sets the stage for a harmonious dance between the known and the unknown.

The tapestry we've crafted together is a mosaic that reflects the multifaceted nature of storytelling in the age of artificial intelligence. From AI-assisted writing to the emergence of multimodal narratives, the threads of innovation, adaptation, and ethical considerations converge into a rich tapestry that adorns the landscape of creative expression.

Writers are the weavers of this tapestry, shaping narratives that bridge the past, present, and future. As they navigate the intricate patterns of technology and creativity, the tapestry unfurls with the promise of a tomorrow where the written word becomes a kaleidoscope of diverse voices, perspectives, and forms.

The dance between human creativity and artificial intelligence is a timeless waltz that transcends the constraints of a single book or exploration. It is a dance that continues beyond these pages, into the writing rooms, studios, and imaginations of authors who dare to push against the boundaries of convention.

As writers, you are the choreographers of this dance, guiding the steps with the finesse of your craft. The intricate footwork of human imagination and the rhythm of machine-generated insights create a dance that is both familiar and unprecedented. The dance continues, inviting writers to embrace the rhythm of innovation and the melody of possibilities.

The horizon before us is a canvas waiting to be painted with the strokes of creativity and the hues of the unknown. In this era where artificial intelligence becomes a companion in the creative process, the unknown is not a daunting abyss, but a canvas filled with endless potential. It is an invitation to explore, to experiment, and to redefine the boundaries of what is conceivable.

As writers venture into the unknown, they carry with them the lessons learned, the insights gained, and the resilience to adapt. The unknown horizon is not a destination but a journey—an ever-unfolding narrative where the stories written today echo into the tomorrows yet to be penned. The echoes of tomorrow beckon writers to dream, to create, and to contribute to the symphony of human expression. As we conclude this exploration, let the echoes linger—an enduring reminder that the narrative continues, the dance endures, and the unknown horizon awaits the footsteps of those who dare to write the stories of tomorrow.